A gift for:

_____

From:

_____

To Mom,

I love you because...

Published by MJF Books
Fine Communications
322 Eighth Avenue
New York, NY 10001

To Mom, I Love You Because…

LC Control Number: 2011942842
ISBN-13: 978-1-60671-124-8
ISBN-10: 1-60671-124-5

This edition is published by MJF Books in arrangement with Red Rock Press.

Book design by Kathy Herlihy-Paoli
Inkstone Design, Inc.

Printed in Singapore

MJF Books and the MJF colophon are trademarks of Fine Creative Media, Inc.

TWP   10   9   8   7   6   5   4   3   2   1

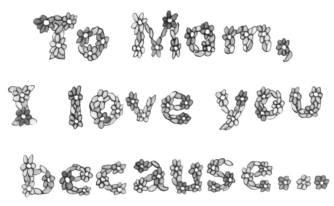

To Mom, I love you because...

Tomoe Sasaki Farley

MJF BOOKS
New York

...you were my personal driver.

...you read me that book over and over again.

...you gave me strength when I needed it.

…*your lap was the best pillow I ever had.*

...you clapped for me.

...you taught me that everything has its place.

...you chased away my bad dreams.

...you made a bath seem like an adventure.

...your hands are warm and soft.

...you fed me with love.

...when the going gets tough you're a match for it.

...you appreciate who I am.

...you were my tutor.

…you made sure I was the warmest kid in the neighborhood.

...you smell good.

...you showed me the world.

...you made me swallow that nasty cough syrup.

...you looked like a queen when you dressed up. And you still reign.

...you never forget my birthday.

…you kept my secret.

…*your kisses made my bruises better.*

...you were my relationship coach.

...you've always believed in me.

...you still care if I eat right.

...your memory is better than any search engine.

...you baby me when I need it.
(and sometimes when I don't).

...the recipes in your head beat the ones in my cookbooks.

...you are what a mom is supposed to be.

...you're my biographer.

...you are as beautiful as ever!